TWO LAUGHS FOR EVERY TEAR

Two Laughs For Every Tear

A Collection of Poems on Life

Robert E. Lee

Copyright © 2022 Robert E. Lee

The moral right of the author has been asserted.

Apart from any fair dealing for the purposes of research or private study, or criticism or review, as permitted under the Copyright, Designs and Patents Act 1988, this publication may only be reproduced, stored or transmitted, in any form or by any means, with the prior permission in writing of the publishers, or in the case of reprographic reproduction in accordance with the terms of licences issued by the Copyright Licensing Agency. Enquiries concerning reproduction outside those terms should be sent to the publishers.

This is a work of fiction. Names, characters, businesses, places, events and incidents are either the products of the author's imagination or used in a fictitious manner. Any resemblance to actual persons, living or dead, or actual events is purely coincidental.

Matador
Unit E2 Airfield Business Park
Harrison Road,
Market Harborough. LE16 7UL
Tel: 0116 279 2299
Email: books@troubador.co.uk
Web: www.troubador.co.uk/matador
Twitter: @matadorbooks

ISBN 978 1803131 085

British Library Cataloguing in Publication Data.
A catalogue record for this book is available from the British Library.

Printed and bound in Great Britain by 4edge Limited
Typeset in 11pt Minion Pro by Troubador Publishing Ltd, Leicester, UK

Matador is an imprint of Troubador Publishing Ltd

PREFACE

Life
Different observations and Living experiences.
Moments where life shows its hand.
Good, bad, happy or sad,
Has this happened to you?
A long journey rekindled,
Many boundaries crossed describing human thoughts feelings and realities.

TICK TOCK

The hands of the clock go round and round.
Many moments without a sound.
The hands turn night into days.
Seconds to minutes, to hours that record many ways.
It's perpetual, silent, no sound.
It sees all lost and found.
It changes darkness into light.
This is a magnificent sight.
It ticks on, always at your beck and call.
In winter, autumn, summer and spring.
It shows us everything.
The clock, slow or fast no lies its true.
The clock is watching over you.

CHURCHILL

You knew when he was in the room,
Shrouds of smoke overshadowed gloom.
That cigar a symbol to all,
His frame robust at beck and call.
Forward only did he go,
To hold Britain against the foe.
A mind like a razor, born to lead,
In our greatest hour of need.
No obstacles, he did his duty,
Our heroic bulldog beauty.
A warrior Churchill to their cost,
His honour cherished, never lost.

GRANDFATHER CLOCK

Standing there with its' face like no other,
Expressionless and without motion.
Winding back of what stories it might tell,
Turning forward what scenarios lie in wait,
From seconds to minutes to hours one can be early or late.
Days become night, the light becomes darkness.
The years pass and still it remains in all entirety.
Its longevity and grace one cannot fail to admire,
Of greater more accurate instruments I know not.
Whilst friendlier nations could run amok.
Great voids of time and space are covered by that
Grandfather clock.

RECONCILIATION

I am working away every month and each day
But I will soon be home and that's ok.
Then we will start talking and we will both have our say.
I have missed our closeness not being able to stay.
We left things rather up in the air.
Perhaps both of us really didn't show enough care.
Soon I will see you again face to face.
How could I ever forget your beauty, poise and grace.
When we meet again I know with each other we will be true.
And I know our love will then again come shining through.

RESCUED

I see angels looking through clouded skies,
At minds in bodies that have no eyes.
A continuing search at perilous souls,
Going nowhere heads with holes.
Ears not listening, mouths wrongly speaking.
Unassuming bodies rapidly creaking.
Torn rejected, having no scope,
The angels will find the ones with hope,
And sit behind them spying.
Their sorrow heeded no more crying.
New pathways will open up their sights,
Shining out like neon lights.
The way will be there for them to follow,
Each willing soul no longer hollow.
Well led for the rest of their days,
Their futures fortuitous in many ways.

MISSING YOU

Today I find myself again at this place
But you are gone, and I no longer see that loving face.
Missing is your pose and grace,
You are gone without a trace.
No more tears no more smiles,
You are missing, seems a million miles.
Perhaps one day you will again be near,
And I can again live with you without any fear.

HOMELESS

I see you there on the street,
Looking shabby and ashen faced.
You are unshaven,
Clothes dishevelled and dirty.
Your hair is tied back it is so long,
The dust on your head is visible.
Your eyes are sunk in.
You have had little sleep.
You share a corner with two older men.
Empty alcohol bottles strewn everywhere.
A shabby woollen blanket barely covers your legs,
Is this what you have become?
A shadow of your former self?
Couldn't you bring yourself to tell me you were homeless?

DOWN OUR STREET

It's all happening down our street.
Some small girls are linking hands and dancing with happy feet.
A boy is kicking a football up against a wall.
A mother cries out to a child.
"Come in your dinner's ready" but they can't hear the call.
A lady passes by and drops her shopping across the floor.
She cries out and gets help from a neighbour quickly coming to the fore.
Empty milk bottles are being put out on someone's step with a rattle
And a ding.
A blackbird perched on top of a tree is starting to sing.
A girl pushes a pram with a baby, going for a walk.
The baby is crying, pity it can't talk.
Two football fans pass by, shouting and waving their scarves,
Above their heads.
A large lorry pulls up making somebody a delivery of beds.
Now some people are dragging out their bin,
And all you can hear is that awful din.
A rushing post-man delivers the post late, he's well out on his feet,
But this is just one of the many things that happen down our street.

SOMEWHERE

I saw your picture in a book I recognised and took another look.
Yes, I saw that we were talking.
On a summer night just walking.
We would go for miles and miles Each of us with a hundred smiles.
Such moments filled with bliss,
Ones that I will surely miss.
You were the apple of my eye I had no time to say goodbye.
I feel that I can no longer do,
Where are you?
I belong with you.

DEPRESSION

I lie still in a darkened room
The walls are closing in
My mind is full of emptiness and sorrow.
I am anxious and afraid,
Unable to change thought.
Tomorrow, tomorrow is another day I must reject all darkness and sorrow.
But my thoughts are so empty and unhappy,
I must involve myself in speech and movement
Carry on pushing and I will survive!

CHOICES

Life is like a vacuum it passes you by
There are many spaces, many faces, visits to many places.
There are many gaps left behind.
Did I do that?
Should I have left it?
Was I kind?
Could I have done better in that job?
Was I right to move, or should I have stayed for a few more bob?
Should I have married or stayed single?
Was my body meant to travel and mingle?
Many do's and don'ts, wills and wont's.
A lot of decisions about jeans and coats.
A lifetime, but you have all the tools.
Don't drift just keep to your rules.

GONE

At the top of the stairs the study is empty
Your ideas and writings are no longer plenty.
Your chair is bare,
There is emptiness and no longer care
The studies you made are no longer there,
You have left us I don't know where.
However, I take comfort in the fact that you still had much to do,
Wherever you are it will be completed because that is you.

THE DISSIDENT

I lay there cooped up,
Too weak to move. I the only furniture.
My time is near,
There is no prayer, no fear.
Bones ached, limbs motionless.
No real feeling.
Pain long gone.
And for what?
The crime,
Freedom.
Speech, choice, time and space,
I wanted it shared, but not them with me.
I will go in darkness, the way of others,
They can take my body,
But not my mind.

DANCE WITH ME

Come dance with me.
Everybody will see.
Movement, all eloquently.
Dance All watched no secrecy.
Room to room, on each floor arm in arm
I adore.
Our dancing coming to the fore.
No separation, together without a care.
All love and beauty laid bare.
Make it real, let them see.
Please come, and dance with me.

DREAMS

Everybody else is dreaming a dream.
That they have been to places that they have never seen.
Landscapes in a far off land,
Pictures in colour to understand.
If you feel that the dream comes true,
You may have been there before and its "déjà vu".
Things may not be what they seem.
But the gift's in your head, so just dream.

ACTING

So you want to be an actor then?
Acting centre stage.
You might be old you might be young,
Go on act your age.
Different voices, choices, clothes to wear,
Plenty make-up wigs, different coloured hair.
So many plots, and many surprises.
Touring places never boring,
Keeping audiences on applauding.
A star on radio even telly,
You may get the bird, even the wellie.
You'll probably live from day to day,
So save your money, put it away.
Endless hours entertaining others,
Many children, fathers, and mothers.
So you want to be an actor when?
Go on be an actor then.

THE LOVE OF MY LIFE

I met you that time in a club,
I knew from that first second it was true love.
We would go out places, see many faces.
You even came to one of those dog races.
I knew from then that you would be my wife,
'Cos you're the love of my life.
All those lazy days just hanging about.
I can't bear the thought of being without.
Many a holiday filled with fun.
And you with your tan from days in the sun.
You're second to none, just being my wife.
'Cos you're the love of my life.

LOST

I look back at days gone by,
Days when you were the apple of my eye.
Almost as if ordained from above,
The two of us were so in love.
Our wedding day was full of bliss
Kiss followed kiss after kiss.
All those days together we bonded like glue.
Then the illness that we never knew,
Slowly, so slowly, you drifted away.
No longer could we talk and have our say,
I grieved and all could see
That I had lost a part of me.

WATER

Clear liquid hardly seen
Add soap it makes you clean.
It flows through the pipes from out of the road,
It's not solid and is bottled cold, It gives life to every tap
But freezes in a cold snap
Water is the staff of life,
But when it leaks it can cause strife.
The fridge makes it turn to ice
Cooling us down till we feel nice.
We get charged for personal use
Free no longer so don't abuse
What's it really worth?
Who cares?
Cheers to the greatest drink on earth

THE SNOWMAN

Standing high in a supreme pose
An orange carrot sticking out for a nose.
Down his chest empty cotton reels painted black.
This snowman is posh, the leader of the pack.
A stripy wool scarf covers his neck.
He's so romantic you could give him a peck.
On top of his head an old bent hat,
Everyone loves him, fancy that!
He can't be bought, he can't be sold,
He's here again as wide as the road.
He doesn't scream or shout,
But you can't fail to notice when he's about.
The children are shouting,
Now "Come and Play".
But the snowman stays quiet, he's nothing to say.
Night-time comes he's still standing high.
Next morning everyone waves as they go by.
If only the snowman could go for a walk.
He would tell plenty of stories and give many a talk.

THE ART OF SLEEP

Passing sleep or lasting sleep
Not even anytime a peep.
Night or day,
You're well away.
Napping an art at length.
Good for health,
No claim to wealth.
At the table a given art, and steady.
Ok, unless the meal is ready.
In bed, waking up now refreshed.
Whilst asleep perhaps we have all been blessed.

IN REMEMBERANCE

You can't put a value on life.
It means so much to a husband or a wife,
To one, and all others.
To the sisters, daughters, sons and brothers.
Our lost grand– parents, and family all.
Let us remember, let us re-call.
Life, value it whilst on this earth.
Respect it, our heroes showed its worth.

ELEVEN

Eleven is a lovely age, short trousers into long.
Looking at the top ten hits and knowing every song.
Learning to comb my hair one way,
But no matter how long I try it never seems to stay.
From primary school to high school stream,
A new blazer in between.
Coming home late, mother shouting where have you been?
That blazer already needs a clean.
Choosing my own clothes, no longer mothers' naff,
No more shouting,
Get out you've been there long enough,
When I'm in my bath.
Being sent down the chippy,
Conscious of my waist-line, so trying to keep nippy.
At the weekend staying up late watching tele,
Mother shouting down at me,
Get those undies in the wash they're starting to get smelly!
Saving up for my first pair of boots,
What a price!
Noticing all the girls in my class are very nice.
Weekend sleepovers at my mates, and staying awake most of the night.
After experimenting with cider, next morning not a pretty sight.
Plenty of class birthday parties going on late.
Now I know how to celebrate
Eleven is a lovely age.

FOGBOUND

Bodies, bodies, in the fog
Chasing shadows, who's who?
Plenty of mystery, no face to face.
People are walking, but where to?
No signs of clear space,
Can't make them out, is it you or you?
No smiling face.
Nobody in view.
Little sound no-one about,
Thicker now, you can't hear a shout.
Can't see them or guess what they're like.
Suddenly movement, fog lifting.
The eyes can see, the bodies are shifting.

A HAPPENING

Last night you appeared to me in a dream.
You were just as you would seem.
So real, nothing out of place,
You looked so young, your body, your face.
You spoke " I am good".
Don't worry here, everything is peaceful and understood.
Is everything with you ok, she asked,
I replied everything is fine this way.
Then suddenly she was no longer there
Gone, nobody , no stare.
As I turned around,
I felt something pass through me with intense heat,
I then awoke, shaky and hot, the dream was so real and I felt spiritually complete.

ME AND THEM

Me and Them.
I hear voices.
Voices From where they come I know not.
But they arrive.
I cannot not stop them.
But they are always there.
Coming and going.
Sometimes they want to do bad.
I need to block them out.
But I cannot.
Day or night they make me feel so sad.
But they will return, from the inner workings of my head.
I need some sort of better control.
Get rid! Get rid!
I tell myself If only I had the key,
I would lock them away forever.

MONEY

Just money.
Money money it's just brass.
Spondoolicks!
It's just cash.
People spend it if a stash.
All that spending.
All that lending.
Young and old some quite posh.
Hard earned all that dosh.
Moulon,or is it quid.
Some even call it squid.
Even known as some boodle, or cheddar it can be chunky.
Hey mate can you spare a monkey?
Money, money, by a name.
No matter what its spent the same.

ADOPTION

They came from all corners of the earth,
Each one will grow and show their worth.
It mattered not from which their seed,
Neither their colour or their creed.
They will all learn and lead.
Each one of them with mouths to feed.
We would educate them and they would learn.
Tiny minds with energy to burn.
Some clever, maybe some not so good.
But they will all be loved and understood.
Adults they will become.
But they may never know who is their Mum.

I'VE GOT A WALRUS

I've got a walrus tied on a lead
He pampers to my every need.
I got a walrus like you've never seen
Wherever I go this walrus has been.
He laughs, he cries
He's got such droopy eyes.
I think he has been sent from above
All he does is show me love
I've got a walrus.

SEARCHING

The boy who fell overboard,
Had bright red hair and sparkling blue eyes.
Bendy legs and chunky thighs.
Remember his laughter and his cry,
He was always to reason why.
Slowly, oh so slowly did he grow,
Everything he wanted to know.
He was wise before his time.
A little professor in his prime.
Now he's become a friend of the sea.
But he will always be part of me.
Please find him.

LOST LOVE

A saddened tear across the eye,
Her long lost love has waved good-bye.
For on the traveller to pastures new.
Behind him love that he once knew.
he will never laugh again or kiss,
Share happy moments with such bliss.
They will never chatter with endless talk,
Lie together, or take a walk.
She cries now to rid the pain,
But her heart will never be the same.

THAT VOICE

I hold onto the phone again and again,
Speaking to an automatic operator and it's a pain.
It makes you sick when you first get on.
You hear if you want, blah, blah, blah, press one,
Or blah, blah, press two or three, or four, by which time I just feel put upon.
But, it goes on and on, for all other blah, blah, blah, press Five.
By which time my brains have taken a dive.
The minutes pass, by now I have had enough of that wretched Voice. It's time to make the only choice.
I press down on the dialling tone.
And have never been so happy to hang up the phone.

PRECIOUS LIGHT

Oh look at you great shining ball,
Up there floating please don't fall.
Like some inflatable balloon,
You are my daunting moon.
Ever shining bright,
You are a night-time light.
No place for you to hide,
No ugliness or better side.
A guardian of the skies.
With an honest face that tells no lies.
Constantly watching over us.
A searching study without a fuss.
No man-made structure can match your sight.
You everlasting perfect light.

DANCE FINAL

Thirty-one, eighteen, twenty-two,
Numbers called, they troop in pairs of two.
In all six pretenders to the crown.
Each contrasts the other, judges sit down.
The dance announced, audience in a trance,
Watching finalists of Latin Dance.
Music strikes up, a Tango then a Rumba, each draws their partner, no time to slumber.
Cheek to cheek they glide.
A shimmer, shake then slide.
Now a Pasodoble, a face up on the floor,
Stomping at each other, a bull and a matador.
Women magnificent with hair slicked back,
Brightly coloured gowns, movement, never slack.
Men eye-catching in dark sequinned suits,
Finesse matched with charm all suave beauts.
Final dance over each bows to applause.
Judges mingle comparing notes, announcements in due course.
Results in reverse order, third, and second receive a prize.
Finally, the winners' ecstatic, emotion in their eyes.
The sash is placed upon them, the trophy's been won.
Exhibition dance foot perfect, never over-done.
The audience applauds sat at tables lit by lamps.
They won't forget a moment, knowing they've seen true champs.

SOMEWHERE

I saw your picture in a book.
I recognised and took another look.
Yes, I saw that we were talking.
On a summer night just walking.
We would go for miles and miles.
Each of us with a hundred smiles.
Such moments filled with bliss.
Ones that I will surely miss.
You were the apple of my eye.
I had no time to say goodbye.
I feel that I can no longer do,
Where are you? I belong with you.

THAT FEELING

Have you ever had that feeling.
You have had a big win and want to walk on the ceiling.
Or you have had one to many and your brains reeling.
Somebody talks to you without any meaning.
You're on a blind date but with whom are you dealing.
You have eaten something, and your stomach says it wasn't appealing.
You have just seen something that is disbelieving.
Your ill, but the doctor says you will soon be healing.
Just moments, have you ever had that feeling?

MARTHAS' CAKE DAY

The oven is heated, the cake tins are ready.
Cream in the butter and sugar, go Martha, steady!
Now in go the eggs.
She whisks together, suddenly a yellow mix,
And she sifts over the flour.
It's time to start right on the hour.
Divided into each cake tin she pours,
Not a drop wasted on those shiny floors.
She times it, a twenty-minute bake.
Times up, she removes them, magic two halves of cake.
Times for the twins to meet each other, and she's upbeat.
Sandwiched together with jam now complete.
Boy oh boy, Martha has done it again and served up a treat.

LEONARD

Oh Leonard, in the corner verily out of sorts,
A penny, a penny, for your downcast Thoughts.
Your pockets so bulging with juvenile delights,
A conker, chewing gum, dirty hankies, all hideous sights.
A face of guilt no longer showing mirth,
No hint of innocence, present at your birth.
When you woke this morning you were feeling fine,
No hint of deliberate deeds, no hint of any crime.
Oh Leonard you are a sinner,
Your only crime in life today was to miss mum's dinner.

I GOTTA HORSE

I gotta a horse.
It will win of course.
He's a little bit thinner.
But a cert winner.
Starters flag up,
Go on my son, go on.
Oh, what a ride.
He's taken it all in his stride.
Passed one horse, then another.
He's out on his own, no need for cover.
The winning post looms just in time.
I gotta a horse and he's all mine.

PAST PARTY

A party all of us seven,
A table full of heaven.
Bridge rolls all flavour,
Sausage rolls awaiting savour.
Sarnies too, each a taste.
Can't let any go to waste.
Trifle and ice cream too.
The finest taste I ever knew.
Now the meringues come.
Don't eat them all, save me some.
Crispy all over, topped with cream,
They are positively obscene.
Joy much joy, without a care,
That's the way we were.
But keep your memories and your smile.
Life will return in just a while.

THE HUNGRY SQUIRREL

Cyril the bushy squirrel comes at four.
The squirrel from the Wirral nestles his nose up
Against our door.
Standing there just like before,
With his wide grey wagging tail,
His crouching stance, has hardly ever known to fail.
The door opens, he is wide – eyed and almost begging.
Once he's had his nibble he's off and starts legging,
Usually into the hole he's burrowed under the fence,
There he goes with one last stare, no recompense.
He will go from house to house, step by step, floor by floor.
We look forward to next time, because we know Cyril will return At Four.

DADDY COOL

My Daddy is so cool.
When he goes to the shop he is no fool.
He's a handyman and knows every tool.
Each night he's watching telly with his feet up on his stool.
He loves horses, he's even rode a mule.
A champion swimmer in the pool,
That's my Daddy he's Daddy cool.

A SUCCESS

The headmaster told Danny he wouldn't amount to much.
And his parents dismayed believed as such.
So he left school with nothing to show.
But to Danny this was not a blow.
Unknown to his Mum and Dad, he had a hidden gift,
This was music, and this gave him a lift.
He saved up his pocket money and bought a guitar.
He just wanted success and to go far.
At first his practising was quite a din Mum and Dad knew it,
The walls were so thin.
Then slowly he mastered his art,
He searched all the music ads for his dream to start.
Then one day he saw an advert for a lead guitar in this group,
They loved him, took him, and now he is part of their loop.
Hit records followed and they were invited to play at the Royal Albert Hall,
It's time to give his old headmaster a call.
Danny invited him to the concert, to show him how wrong he had been.
Now Danny was so successful it had to be seen.
At the end of the concert he shook Danny's hand, and apologised For saying he wouldn't go far.
Especially now Danny's a successful star.

BATHTIME BLUES

Baby Joel is in his tub
Waiting for his cleansing scrub.
He splashes with his sponge up and down,
Don't do that says his Mum, giving him a frown.
He scowls and turns on his tum,
I need to do your neck now, stop having fun.
He splashes on and lies so low Come on,
Mum says let me make you glow Joel wades up and down his bath.
Giving Mum a right old laugh.
Now it's time to fetch him out.
Joel stands up and cries and starts to shout.
Listen baby, mum says it's time to get you dry
So you better behave and stop that cry
Now dry, on comes the powder
He smells clean, bath-time over, and Mum couldn't be any prouder.

SPARKY

Charlie Sparks the leccy man, a wizard at his game.
He knew the name of every wire, to me there are all the same.
No longer an apprentice, a master of his trade.
Now in business he made sure he was well paid.
Floors in houses, cookers, and every light.
Sparky, with his helmet and overalls on, was a happy sight.
All the housewives would flutter their eyelashes when he came through their doors.
But he was just their smiling saviour and there to wire their floors.
Where Sparky went he was followed by his cables.
He even wired a barn once, whilst the horse was in his stables.
Oh Sparky, you are brill wiring up, with sockets in every hall.
Sparky the leccy man is available to one and all.

THE POND

The midday sun shines across the face of the pond
All is silent here in the back of beyond.
An army of reeds stand to attention
Water lilies in between, too many to mention.
A surround of colour all around.
A scene of white, and purple and green.
Not one note of sound.
All complement the pond, all must be seen.
Here come the ducks, they waddle one behind the other,
No misbehaving here, in line behind the mother.
Behind them an occasional ripple across the pond.
Those ducks dare not abscond.
Now a visitor, the afternoon frog jumps in,
Almost expecting him, the goldfish unimpressed, turn the other way and swim.
There is much to admire in the daily life of the pond,
Much beauty of which I fond.

JUST ONE OF THOSE THINGS

It's just one of those things.
Have you ever seen a bird that never sings
Or a bell that never dings It's just one of those things.
A telephone that never rings It's just one of those things.
A table-tennis ball that never pings
A lady wearing many rings It's just one of those things.
A bee that never stings
An opera singer that never sings
It's just one of those things.
A dog trained to fetch but never brings
Chinese vases that can never be mings
It's just one of those things.
A man playing a guitar with only two strings
It's just one of those things.

THAT'S LIFE

Mother's playing bingo down the old folk's hall
Wondering will the next one be her lucky ball.
The caller's shouting "two fat ladies" eighty-eight,
She shrieks, who are you calling fat my mate?
Father's out the back of the house mowing the lawn,
He couldn't sleep, he's been awake since dawn.
Their son is in his room on another computer game,
He's sure he will be a winner and his name will end in fame.
His sister always upstairs playing the beauty queen,
The make-up like the brightest coloured picture you've ever seen.
Nan is doing the supper, the biggest meal,
She's ever so keen!
And if you're late she will quiz, where you've been.
The decorator's busy mucking up the hall,
Fancy wallpaper hanging wall to wall.
The dog, now he's the clever one, he's gone out for the day,
He's having a good bark when strangers come his way.
Just a normal household functioning again,
That's life in all its glory, thank god it's still the same.

For exclusive discounts on Matador titles,
sign up to our occasional newsletter at
troubador.co.uk/bookshop